~~UN~~COMFORTABLE
IN
BUSSINESS

An Introverts Guide To Be Highly

Effective In Bussiness

By

Cherise L. Allen, MBA

Contents

About The Author 1

Chapter 1 Starting from the Bottom: Putting the work in 3

Chapter 2 Interviewing: Dos and Don'ts 5

Chapter 3 Requirements: What you need for this industry 7

Chapter 4 Building a Team: It's all about trust 9

Chapter 5 Gaining Confidence: Fake it 'til you make it 11

Chapter 6 Public Speaking: Say it like you mean it 13

Chapter 7 Dressing the part: Dress for the job you want 15

Chapter 8 Getting Results: Enacting your influence 17

SUMMARY OF CONCEPTS 19

ABOUT THE AUTHOR

My name is Cherise Allen, a Masters of Business Administration graduate and former Regional Manager at the largest c-store chain in the world. This is my playbook to becoming a leader in the retail industry. My journey hasn't always been easy. As a driven young black woman, climbing to the heights that I have managed to was only that much harder.

It took grit, strength, and an iron will to get me to where I am today. If you feel like retail is the space that you're meant to be in, or if you've been searching for that motivation to get you to new heights in your career, this book is for you.

As someone who has always been innately reserved and introverted, going after my goals in a field where the loudest and most charismatic voice in the room often gets the promotions, I know just how much of a spiritual and mental stretch it might be for many of you out there today.

From my early days as an assistant store manager at one of largest retail pharmaceutical companies in the country Rite Aid Pharmacy, and my climb to official store manager, to my strides for district manager and most recent position regional manager; I'll be taking you through the tricks of the trade that you'll need to climb your way to the very top.

For that woman of color that is doing her best to swim against the current in a white, male dominated industry, here's what I have to say to you: don't give up, don't give in, and don't you ever back down. Let your professionalism and your experience speak for itself, but don't forget to go after what you want and advocate for yourself.

Hard work and an unwavering faith in God are what got me through some of the most difficult moments in this journey. If you can place your trust in God, give Him the glory and take heed of the advice that I have for you, I have no doubt in my mind that you'll make it to any career destination that you deserve.

Take it from the woman who began her journey on the frontlines in customer service as a retail clerk at Claire's Accessories, and who has gone on to oversee 81 convenience stores, managing 8 field consultants at 7Eleven, and sixteen in shop luxury boutiques across Pennsylvania, New York, New Jersey, and Virginia for LXR & Co a Canadian resale luxury company. With recruiting, payroll, partnership, and sales management responsibilities across the board, my role is not an easy one, but it's one that I have found fulfillment in having a passion for people and this industry.

This is your career, and this is your life. If you're ready to take the next step in your career, allow me walk you through the steps that you'll need to take in order to advance your way to new heights.

Chapter 1

Starting from the Bottom: Putting the work in

When people say that they're willing to put in the work, start from the bottom, and push their way through to the height of their careers, it's often just smoke and mirrors. Very few people actually know what it takes to make it up the corporate ladder. What I can tell you for certainty is this, you have to have that leadership mindset from the word go.

In 2001, I began my educational journey at Bloomsburg University, earning my Bachelor of Science in Business Administration by the summer of 2005. I've always maintained a self-motivated attitude in life, and I find that having the right attitude will take you a lot further than having a negative one. As the Varsity Athletics Captain at the time, the determination that I had to have on the field, taught me so much about the determination that I would have to have in business. The truth is, life is not always going to go according to plan, and there will be seasons of drought before you can begin to receive the rains that will grow you. You need to be capable of holding on during those drought periods. You need to have the determination and the resilience to bounce back when things get tough. It's a characteristic that I often looked for, and tried to cultivate, during my time as a mentor for incoming freshmen.

There is no shortcut to success, but there is a blueprint. As they say, opportunity is often overlooked because it presents itself as hard work in overalls. That, however, is exactly where you need to be in your early days. You need to be willing to start from the bottom and genuinely put in the work. No matter how educated you are, or how intelligent you think you may be, if you're not willing to listen, learn, and work your way up, you're going to be selling yourself short.

I'll let you in on a human resource secret. Most recruiters are not looking for the most accredited individual in the room, they're looking for the person who is willing to provide the business with quality input without having to be asked, coerced, or followed around. They're looking for the person who can take initiative and remain disciplined in demanding situations. They are looking for confidence with a touch of humility.

My first industry related job involved a lot of frontline work. As an assistant store manager, providing consistent customer service made up a good deal of my role in the earlier months. Having to project my positive, and friendly demeanor, despite being incredibly introverted was a challenge that I had to overcome. My team needed me to lead by example and to motivate them towards achieving excellence in their daily tasks.

It's vital that you acknowledge that you are still on the ladder when you're getting started. Despite the fact that you might be managing a team and an array of administrative responsibilities, having an inflated ego about it is not going to get you to where you need to be. Leadership by any means is cultivated through earned respect and hard work. There is no place for entitlement in this stage, or any other for that matter. Roll up your sleeves and get to work!

The humble will see their God at work and be glad. Let all who seek God's help be encouraged. Psalm 69:32

Chapter 2

Interviewing: Dos and Don'ts

When it comes to interviewing there are so many proverbial booby traps that people walk right into. The same old answers are played out and are not going to gain you the good favor that you need in order to win a new and improved role. The great news for businesses is that there is a variety of talent in the human resources pool right now. The bad news for those looking for a new and exciting role is that interviewers are becoming desensitized to typical interview answers. Saying things like *"I'm a motivated self-starter"*, or any other cliché lines that they've heard thousands of times before, is going to make you a number to them and nothing more. I know that it sounds quite negative, but I want you to succeed, so honesty is definitely the best policy right now. Before I get ahead of myself, let's start off right at the beginning; getting dressed to impress.

When it comes to the right dress-code for an interview, you definitely don't want to walk in adorning your casual attire. You're a budding business woman. You might even be the next CEO of that very company, so dress like it. Wear a comfortable heel, nothing too high. You want to be able to walk and move confidently. If you're shaky on your feet, or feeling squeezed into a tight and unimaginably high pair of heels, your focus is going to shift from your presentation to your physical appearance - and yes, there is a distinct difference between the two. Your dress code speaks to your persona and makes a statement. Your physical appearance on the other hand, has practically nothing to do with your business persona or this interview. Dress to impress, but be true to the image that you are going to be bringing to the arena each day. When you're true to yourself in these situations, it allows you to engage with the interviewer in a more authentic way. When you're putting on a show, you're going to mess up and forget your lines.

Next on your agenda should be how you answer those oh-so-important interview questions. Remember, be true to who you are but try to steer clear of negative self-speak. For instance, a common question that comes up in interviews is: *'What would you say your core weakness is?'*

Instead of saying something like, 'I tend to be quite reserved around new people', try saying, 'I tend to observe a situation quite extensively before providing an opinion. Speeding up this process is something that I'm working on, but it's part of my nature to listen and observe before I speak.' This tells the interviewer that if they find you to be a little reserved in your early days, you are not being aloof, but are assessing your position amongst the team.

Be honest, but put a positive spin on everything that they ask about you. Do that, and I can assure you that you'll be getting call backs from the majority of the companies that you've interviewed with. Another best practice is to find commonalities with the interviewer. Some of my best interviews had been due to finding topics that you have in common. For example, I interviewed for my most recent position at 7 Eleven and I was in the third round of interviews, I was asked about my reason for working for the LXRandCo, the luxury resale company. For anyone who knows me, they know I love a good luxury handbag, working for this company felt like home. The interviewer mentioned his wife loves luxury handbags and based on that we spoke for sometime about the various products, resale values etc. So the point is it's always good to have common topics to build trust and sometimes convey your excitement and expertise with the interviewer.

In quietness and in confidence shall be your strength. Isaiah 30:15

Chapter 3

Requirements: What you need for this industry

Once you have your foot in the door, you need to hone the skills that you need to make it in this industry. It's not enough to have the qualifications, or even a bit of experience. What is going to set you apart are your soft skills. These are skills that you can develop if they don't come naturally to you. Yes, having the knowledge of how to complete the technical elements of your administrative role is important. However, having the skills needed to bring all of those elements together and run a tight ship is a different ball game altogether.

Leadership skills are incredibly important for this business management role. Leadership that is of any merit is that which doesn't force people to follow. When your team is able to naturally gravitate towards you for answers, and when they feel led by example as opposed to being ruled with an iron fist, you will have cultivated an effective leadership style. To do this you need to show passion for your work and compassion for your colleagues. Focus on your team's wins – cheering publicly. Correct your team's failures – guiding privately. To be a leader you need to be able to inspire the desire to strive for excellence amongst your team. You need to be civic minded; showing your team that you are concerned with their wellbeing and career success.

Communication is going to be paramount for your role. In this industry if you're unable to communicate effectively, you are not going to be able to get very far. It is why I had to make the conscious decision to overcome my own introverted nature. It is imperative that you are able to communicate in a verbal, non-verbal, and written manner as accurately as possible. Where matters of deadlines, inventories, human resource issues, and compliance issues dominate a good chunk of your work time in any given year, being able to communicate and ensure execution in a timely manner is significant in the grand scheme of things.

Innovation is next on the agenda, and I've already touched on this quite briefly. Your higher ups are only going to open the proverbial door in the floor for you to climb up behind them if you are showing initiative and being innovative in your work. If you would like a career where you are told what to do and that is what you do day-in-day-out for the duration of your time with a given company, then this is not the field for you. This field requires you to show your team what you're made of. Handle the tasks that have been laid out in your contract, but don't just do the bare minimum. If you want to get ahead, you have to look at every aspect of your role in relation to business operations and find ways of optimizing it. Make waves, so to speak.

As you begin innovating and growing a pattern of leadership, you'll need to switch your focus more intently towards your team. You cannot do it all on your own. You need the help of those around you. Building a trusting and mutually respectful relationship with your team is going to have you feeling fulfilled and running a successful operation.

For God has not given us a spirit of fear,

but of power and of love and of a sound mind. 2 Timothy 1:7

Chapter 4

Building a Team: It's all about trust

Building a team, and building trust within that team, is no easy task, but it is arguably the most vital aspect for the success of any operation. You are not going to make your way to the top without your team. In a world where we are thankfully becoming more accountable for our actions in all realms of our lives, stepping on people's heads doesn't take you to the top anymore. To be quite frank, the industry is better off for it. Bear in mind that there are still some sharks out there that will try to undercut you, but you need to focus on your leadership style and making real contributions to the livelihoods of your team. There is no joy and no glory in living a life stepping on the heads and toes of others in order to advance your own agendas or desires.

First off, when you begin building a team, you need to have a clearly defined purpose for the team itself and for each member within that team. Having unclear roles and goals will only lead to confusion, work dissatisfaction and resentment. It's one of the easiest ways to create a revolving door of staff who are constantly quitting. Having to hire and train new staff on a continual basis means that you're losing out on precious operation time, and thus revenue.

One thing that my time as a mentor for incoming new employees taught me, is that in order to appeal to the better nature of those you are leading, or mentoring, is to take an interest in helping them to build their confidence in completing their assignment. That is how you build trust. Look, work is work at the end of the day, and many might argue that they are working to earn a living wage and not to make friends. I have a newsflash for those people. We spend approximately **thirty percent** of our lives working. A whole third of our lives! Do you really want to be spending that much time in a position where you, or those around you, are unfulfilled or unhappy? So, take an interest. Get to know one another. Celebrate the wins. Reward the people that you can see are genuinely going above and beyond for the team, but don't ostracize the team members that are not doing as well. Instead of trying to fix their weak spots, find their strengths and help them flourish in that arena.

Finally, treat your team with common decency. There are few things worse than a manager that raises their voice towards, or belittles, their team. If there is a genuine problem with one or more team members, address it early on to ensure that there is not progressive build up of frustration towards them. Remember, it's your job to lead, so be constructive in your approach and give them the decency to address a potentially embarrassing moment in the privacy of an office: one-on-one.

You want to develop a collaborative spirit amongst your team; that perfectly balanced place where roles and expectations seem to spill over from one individual to the next. When there is a good chemistry between team members and a genuine enjoyment for the work that they're doing, they'll naturally want to do more for one another. In the fiscal world, this is going to have you reaching your targets consistently and practically effortlessly. In the spiritual and emotional world, this is going to make being at work so much more enjoyable and you will feel a sense of divine purpose in what you do.

You need to have the confidence to reach that point. For many of us, maintaining true intrinsic self-confidence is easier said than done.

A man takes joy in a fitting reply—and how good is a timely word! Proverbs 15:23

Chapter 5

Gaining Confidence: Fake it 'til you make it

Confidence is a tricky subject. As somebody who is quite introverted, I wouldn't say that I lacked confidence. On the contrary, I was quite confident in my abilities and the guidance that the Lord had given in terms of using those abilities. However, I just wasn't one for large groups, or public speaking. My heart was content with engaging on a one-on-one level, and within small trust-focused teams.

So, this is where the confusion lies for many people. Your willingness to be outgoing might not have much to do with your self-confidence, but the world might perceive it to be. It's your job to make sure that these two elements are not exclusively linked in the way your higher ups, your peers, or your team perceive you. Moreover, don't let it affect how you perceive yourself.

Confidence is not about garnering attention or being center stage. There is a quiet confidence that comes from being well-versed in your role, and knowledgeable in your field. Here's the thing, when you're just starting out, you are going to feel a little uncertain of your capabilities, and this will be a recurring feeling almost every time you level up. It's natural. You need to give yourself the time to adjust. You might begin to question your abilities to take on more intense responsibilities and the pressure might chisel away at your confidence, but I need you to take a long hard look at how far you've come. Just picking up this book is a testament to the fact that you are committed to creating a framework for your career and your life that you have long envisioned.

God has got you. The people around you, including those that are higher up on the ladder than you, are people just like you. They all have fears, hopes, dreams, and aspirations. If they seem like they have a handle on absolutely everything and haven't got a care in the world, that is only because they have been through enough to feel confident that they can navigate whatever their jobs throw at them. That's the only way to create the calm within yourself which you will need to foster self-confidence. You need to tell yourself that failure is inevitable. Mistakes are inevitable. As long as you are giving your best in all that you do and you address mistakes if, and when, they arise, you will be just fine.

Create a routine for yourself. Put on your favorite song while you're getting ready for work each morning; For me depending on the day this can be an uplifting gospel song or my favorite hip hop music. For you, it should definitely be something that makes you feel fierce enough to take on anything that the day has in store for you. You have to actively and consciously find ways to keep yourself motivated. If you can do that, you can keep a consistent level of self-confidence throughout your career. Even people with the greatest support systems need to be able to pick themselves up. It is only through your confidence and your will to persevere that you will keep moving forward.

Relax, remember your purpose, and trust that everything will work itself out as long as you are putting in the work that you are capable of putting in. After all, in the words of Maya Angelou, ***nothing works, unless you do.***

let the wise listen and gain instruction, and the discerning acquire wise counsel. Proverbs 1:5

Chapter 6

Public Speaking: Say it like you mean it

Public speaking is a huge part of leading a team as well as with regards to addressing the necessary partners and stakeholders at a regional and executive level. This was always a biggie for me. Overcoming my need to go inwards, I had to learn to be outspoken. There is a subtle art to public speaking, and it has a lot more to do with the way in which you engage with yourself than it has to do with what you say. Speaking from a place of experience is always going to come off better than making a choreographed speech. Have you ever heard of the saying; *'when it's the truth, you won't have to remember it'?* Keep that in mind when it comes to engaging in public speaking. If you are able to connect what you're trying to say to something that you've experienced and create a link between the two, you'll find it far easier to talk to your audience. That's all that public speaking is when it's all said and done – talking to your audience, and waiting for cues that your message is being well received.

Know this, if you are not particularly good at public speaking and you have something of that nature coming up on your agenda, you are most likely going to bomb a little, and that's ok! The more you put yourself out there, and the more you speak from honest experience, the more you are going to be able to watch for those cues amongst the audience that will help you to adapt on your feet.

That being said, there are steps that you can take to ensure that you are well prepared and confident for your next public speaking affair. Accepting that being nervous and stammering are perfectly normal if you are not used to public speaking is your first step. Your next step is getting to know the people you are addressing. If you're heading out for a shop visit, for example, and there has been word of employee lag or dissatisfaction, then you need to address that. Speak to their good nature, not to their failures. If you're going to be addressing the local team, then you need to come in to speak as an ally. Think back to work experiences where you may not have felt as satisfied as you would have liked to at the time. What are the words you wished someone would have said to you? How would you have been able to open up about your grievances?

Moving on to larger, more corporate audiences, which may include company stakeholders, you need to prepare your material. Try to keep it just as real and honest as you would have done with the aforementioned team, but change up your approach. The takeaway here should be that knowing your audience is crucial to the outcome of your speaking affair. Don't be afraid to use humorous, personal stories to break up the seriousness of the matters which you may be addressing.

Ultimately, you need to know your message, your audience, and your method of delivery. When you're well prepared, you'll be in a better position to open up the opportunity for constructive feedback.

For I, the Lord your God, hold your hand; it is I who say to you, Fear not, I am the one who helps you. Isaiah 41:13

Chapter 7

Dressing the part: Dress for the job you want

I've addressed your dress code during the interview stage, but your dress sense is equally important throughout your career. In the words of bestselling author, Austin Kleon, *'You have to dress for the job you want, not the job you have.'* If you want to climb that corporate ladder, you need to look and act the part. I'm not saying you need to fit in with the masses, or change any aspect of who you are. I'm saying you need to take that personal image and bump it up to one hundred. Walk like a boss, talk like a boss, and dress like a boss.

Not only does dressing to impress let others know that you are a force to be reckoned with, it gives you the confidence to stand tall and command the room; not with words, but with your presence. You are important. Tell yourself that. Feel it, and act accordingly. That's not to say that you should be arrogant in your dress sense or your demeanor, but you should carry yourself with pride.

We have been preconditioned to accept that a suit means someone holds some form of authority or importance. It is for this very specific psychological reason that when you dress like the corporate powerhouse that you are capable of becoming, people will automatically think that you already are. Whether we care to admit it or not, we are constantly making critical assumptions about the world around us based on what we can hear and see. This is no different when it comes to the people we work with. How you dress, as well as how you carry yourself, is constantly being adjudicated by the people around you.

There are very few work environments where what you wear doesn't really matter, but this is not one of them. You need to ensure that you're putting your best foot forward and being noticed by your team and, more especially, your higher ups, for all the right reasons.

When you've got the confidence, the dress sense, and the right attention, it's time to start getting the results.

So do not throw away your confidence; it holds a great reward. Hebrews 10:35

Chapter 8

Getting Results: Enacting your influence

In order for you to get results in this industry you need to focus on goals. It's imperative that you set on creating SMART goals for yourself and each of the departments under your administration. SMART goals are those which are specific, measurable, attainable, relevant and timely. The point of this is to ensure that you are meeting your targets successfully. When you work on measurable goals and focus on data-driven decision making, you're able to save time and get the results that you're after.

Don't be afraid to delegate. Remember, you cannot do it all on your own. There is no point in building a team that you can trust if you can't depend on them to get the job done without you hovering over them. Don't micro-manage, and don't be the helicopter mom of the office world. Hand out tasks that you know your team is fully capable of handling, and then actually let them handle it.

Keep a clearly visible digital or physical record of upcoming deadlines, collaborative projects and important dates. Know which goals are easily attainable and which are more long term, and then visually prioritize them so that everyone on your team is simultaneously working towards a common goal. Give praise where it's due and you'll give yourself the gift of influence amongst your team.

Once you've got the organizational structure in place to make your operations run smoother, you can shift your sights to really maximizing your influence. Be understanding of the people that you work with, at all levels. Make yourself an emotional resource and maintain an open-door policy; whether literally or figuratively. Allow your team to feel safe with you and share some vulnerability in turn. People listen to people who listen to them. If you want to enact your influence you need to learn how to be charismatic and how to be a good listener. Become a mirror for that which people want to see. Become a source of encouragement and healing. More importantly, become the type of person whom you would allow to have influence over yourself.

There are three elements to truly enacting influence and those are retribution, reciprocity, and reasoning. The best of three is reciprocity. It allows you to enact your influence based on mutual respect and exchange with the person whom you are trying to influence. Retribution is based on driving fear into your counterpart, while reasoning is based on persuasion which can be perceived as coercion.

In order to truly get the results that you're after, you need to focus on your goals, measure your success, be data-driven, and enact your influence.

In the same way, let your light shine before others, that they may see your good deeds and glorify your Father in heaven. Matthew 5:16

SUMMARY OF CONCEPTS

In order to get to where you want to be, you have to work your way up from the bottom. There is no substitute for hard work. You are going to have to embrace the notion that hard work is the only real tool to get you to the top.

There are a plethora of dos and don'ts that you should keep in mind on your corporate journey. Everything from the way that you answer interview questions to the way you dress is going to be scrutinized from the moment you decide to venture off into business administration.

Regional retail management is not for the faint of heart. The mindset that you need to adopt for this industry is one rooted in deep self-confidence and self-motivation. It will help you to connect with your peers, deliver impactful messages via public speaking, and build teams that can depend on you as well as on one another.

Once you've learned how to leverage your influence and advocate for your best interests, the world will be at your fingertips. Have faith in yourself and Almighty God, and you will persevere all the way to the heights that you deserve. Thank you for reading.

For I know the plans I have for you, declares the LORD, plans to prosper you and not to harm you, to give you a future and a hope. Jeremiah 29:11

Made in United States
North Haven, CT
21 October 2022

25749081R00015